JUST
· *say* ·
YES!

PARTICIPANT GUIDE

Other Abingdon Press Resources by Robert Schnase

Five Practices of Fruitful Living

Five Practices of Fruitful Congregations

Seven Levers: Missional Strategies for Conferences

Just Say Yes! Unleashing People for Ministry

Just Say Yes! Leader Guide

Just Say Yes! Devotional

Just Say Yes! DVD

Author of *Five Practices of Fruitful Congregations*

Robert Schnase
with Angela Olsen

JUST *say* YES!

UNLEASHING PEOPLE FOR MINISTRY

PARTICIPANT GUIDE

 Abingdon Press™

Nashville

JUST SAY YES! PARTICIPANT GUIDE:
UNLEASHING PEOPLE FOR MINISTRY

ISBN: 978-1-5018-2528-6

16 17 18 19 20 21 22 23 24 25—10 9 8 7 6 5 4 3 2 1
MANUFACTURED IN THE UNITED STATES OF AMERICA

Contents

Introduction to the *Just Say Yes!* Study

Thank you so much for reading *Just Say Yes! Unleashing People for Ministry* by Robert Schnase. This book highlights how church people and church culture often default to *No* rather than *Yes*. Many leaders and congregations struggle with stifling atmospheres of resistance. These cultures continually say *No* to new ideas and to people who are answering God's call to use their gifts and talents. Passionate and creative people sometimes become so frustrated they leave the church. But a different way of being and doing church is possible. That is what this study and the subsequent devotional are all about. To go even further, your church is encouraged to do the four-week *Just Say Yes! Sermon and Worship Series* and the companion four-week *Just Say Yes! Devotional* for congregants; these resources are available online.

This small group study is designed to help you and others in your congregation build on the ideas you've read about in *Just Say Yes!* The aim of this study is to offer you tools to encourage a permission-giving culture in your church. Permission-giving churches recognize that all people have calls to ministry. People in these churches celebrate one another's gifts, dreams, and passions. They encourage each other in ministry. That is the direction this study will take you.

The study is organized into three major themes: Uncover the *Nos*, Unlock the Power of *Yes*, and Unleash a Culture of *Yes*. As you go through the material you will develop in new ways. First, as an individual leader and then, together with others in your congregation, you will begin to develop ideas for creating a culture of fruitfulness for your entire church. This intentional movement from personal to church systems is rooted in the following sentences in *Just Say Yes!*: "Congregations and operational systems never become more permission-giving than the people who lead them. Leaders have a disproportionate influence on the culture and content of a church, and on the processes that either restrain or multiply ministries" (93).

This *Just Say Yes!* study experience will foster your development as a permission-giving leader and equip you to be part of unleashing others for ministry so that yours can become a permission-giving church.

One important note about the study: The material is organized here in three sessions, but it is designed to be flexible so that groups may use it in whatever timeframe works best in their particular context. Your group may be working through the study in three sessions, as one long session, or in smaller increments. Your group leader should explain to you how your group will go through the material before you begin.

In This Book: Small Group Study Guide, Devotional, and Next Steps

This study is designed for use with church councils, staff teams, committee chairs, ministry team leaders, and the like. This participant guide is a complete workbook for participants in the Just Say Yes! group experience and contains everything you should need to participate, in addition to your Bible and a copy of the main book, *Just Say Yes!* The guide includes prompts to reinforce what you learn, questions for reflection and discussion, and specific action steps for becoming permission-giving leaders in the church. It includes plenty of room for writing and note taking during the group experience. The group experience includes six inspiring and compelling videos from real church settings. Several additional video clips are also available for groups wanting to spend more time exploring ideas together.

At the back of this book you'll find the seven-segment devotional. You are strongly encouraged to journey through the devotional on your own after you complete the small group study. The devotional will deepen your experience of the study, and you will find yourself becoming a permission-giving leader. Through this devotional time, the Holy Spirit will empower you to help your congregation toward becoming a permission-giving church.

At the back of this book you'll also find a list of ideas for next steps. These ideas will help you begin thinking about actions to take based upon your new understanding of the permission-giving church. Next steps will help you and other leaders in your church put the rubber to the road.

To Go Deeper: Four-Week Sermon and Worship Series and Four-Week Devotional

For churches and leaders who want to go deeper, a four-week *Just Say Yes! Sermon and Worship Series* is available as a free download online. It includes sermon outlines, prayers, and other liturgical texts for each week—including ideas for conducting the series. This series is a great way to bring the entire congregation on board after groups have first completed the small group study.

A printed four-week *Just Say Yes! Devotional* is also available. It can be used by individual church members autonomously or (ideally) used by every member as a personal study guide accompanying the *Just Say Yes! Sermon and Worship Series*. The material is flexible and accessible for all adult readers and can be done in one sitting or spread throughout the week.

Faith is the reality of what we hope for, the proof of what we don't see.

—Hebrews 11:1

Group Study Sessions

You are the light of the world. A city on top of a hill can't be hidden. Neither do people light a lamp and put it under a basket. Instead, they put it on top of a lampstand, and it shines on all who are in the house. In the same way, let your light shine before people, so they can see the good things you do and praise your Father who is in heaven.

—Matthew 5:14-16

Session 1

Uncover the *Nos*

An unrelenting culture of No *is a contradiction to our sacrament of baptism, stifling hope, new birth, and a sense of God's promise for the future. (x)*

Opening Prayer

[Say in unison] Faithful and life-giving God, please create in this room a sacred space filled with your Holy Spirit. We come here to learn more about you and your call to lead in this church. Open our hearts and minds to the work we must do to honor you. Reveal to us the stifling impact *Nos* have on the gifts, talents, creativity, and passion of your people. Help us feel your grace in moments of conviction and then offer grace to each other through this work. Give us courage to follow you from *No* to *Yes*. By the end of our time together, help us each to say boldly *Yes* Lord, *Yes*! It is in the name of our savior, Jesus Christ, we pray. Amen.

Introductions

We are going to take a few minutes to make sure everyone knows each other. Let's go around the room: share your name and why you said *Yes* to being here today.

Video: *"Just Say Yes! Introductory Video"*

Bishop Robert Schnase shares how *Just Say Yes! Unleashing People for Ministry* can offer hope for those people whose passion has been simmering for years.

Stories of *No*

In addition to these stories of *No*, were there any that really struck you from the book? Take a moment to imagine what these *No* scenarios do to the life of a congregation. How do you feel when you are told *No*?

Checklist of Nos

Take a few moments to check all the types of *Nos* you have received personally as well as all the types of *Nos* you have said yourself. If you want more details about the *Nos* listed, please feel free to reread the section in the book on pages 3–8.

- ❏ You're Not the Pastor
- ❏ I Don't Need That, So Why Should We Do It?
- ❏ Only Five People Signed Up
- ❏ They're Not Our Members Anyway
- ❏ That's Our Room
- ❏ That Will Never Work Here (and I'll See That It Doesn't!)
- ❏ They Can Just Join Us
- ❏ Analysis Paralysis
- ❏ You're Too Young, Too New, or Too Different
- ❏ You're Doing It All Wrong
- ❏ You Didn't Ask Me First
- ❏ Don't Rock the Boat
- ❏ Things Won't Be the Same
- ❏ Others (fill in the blank with your own category) _____

Group Sharing

Describe one of the times you were on the receiving end of a *No* response. What happened to your ministry idea? Have you ever been the one saying *No*? What happened to that ministry idea?

Faulty Assumptions Leading to *No*

1. *This Is Our Church*

Instead of being centered on Christ, we forget we are Christ's body. "When we act as if the church belongs to us—the pastor, the staff, the leaders, the members—then the criteria for why we say *Yes* or *No* becomes what *we* prefer, what *we* want, what *we* seek" (8).

2. *Ideas Come from the Center*

Instead of allowing people to discover unmet needs in the community and encouraging them to develop a ministry, church systems and people say *No*, the ideas have to come from core leadership in the church. "The assumption that ideas must begin at the center and be controlled from the center fosters a tendency to say *No* to new ideas that come from anywhere else" (9).

3. *It's All about Us*

Instead of asking, "What is God calling us to do?" we more often ask, "What's in it for me?" We also ask, "'What will I have to do? What will it cost me?' This natural and understandable response limits mission, stifles creativity, and squelches the genuine call of God" (10).

Group Exercise

Shout out the word or words that come to mind when you hear the following three questions. Our volunteer will record them on the board.

- What happens when we say "This is OUR church"?
- What happens when we believe ideas only come from our core leadership team, "the center"?
- What happens when we say "It's all about me"?

7

Scripture Readings

Matthew 22:34-40

Matthew 25:34-39

Matthew 28:19-20

In light of Jesus's words, what words need to be replaced on the board?

How do these words from our savior change the assumptions?

Before we take a break, please write down one of the *No* scenarios you have experienced—either said or received. These scenarios will be used in the subsequent sessions, so this step is important!

_____

_____

_____

_____

_____

_____

_____

_____

_____

_____

_____

_____

_____

_____

_____

_____

_____

_____

When the Pharisees heard that Jesus had left the Sadducees speechless, they met together. One of them, a legal expert, tested him. "Teacher, what is the greatest commandment in the Law?"

He replied, "You must love the Lord your God with all your heart, with all your being, and with all your mind. This is the first and greatest commandment. And the second is like it: You must love your neighbor as you love yourself. All the Law and the Prophets depend on these two commands."

—Matthew 22:34-40

"Then the king will say to those on his right, 'Come, you who will receive good things from my Father. Inherit the kingdom that was prepared for you before the world began. I was hungry and you gave me food to eat. I was thirsty and you gave me a drink. I was a stranger and you welcomed me. I was naked and you gave me clothes to wear. I was sick and you took care of me. I was in prison and you visited me.'

"Then those who are righteous will reply to him, 'Lord, when did we see you hungry and feed you, or thirsty and give you a drink? When did we see you as a stranger and welcome you, or naked and give you clothes to wear? When did we see you sick or in prison and visit you?'"

—Matthew 25:34-39

"Therefore, go and make disciples of all nations, baptizing them in the name of the Father and of the Son and of the Holy Spirit, teaching them to obey everything that I've commanded you. Look, I myself will be with you every day until the end of this present age."

—Matthew 28:19-20

Session 2

Unlock the Power of Yes

When I'm asked whether I think we should go forward with an idea, if I don't monitor myself to focus on the larger mission, my default response reflects my personal preference and my perception of the impact that the decision will have on me. (10)

Video: A New Way of Being: Sturgeon UMC

The story of Sturgeon United Methodist Church was all too common: too small, too old, too tired. Under the unifying direction of Rev. Mike Will, they joined forces with the four other local churches and forged a new way of being church to their broader community.

Intentional Leadership Reflection

As leaders, do we bring negativity or hope?

_____

_____

_____

_____

Do we bring fear or joy?

_____

_____

_____

_____

Are we staying connected with the one who called us into leadership?

_____

_____

_____

_____

_____

How can we discern if we are knowingly and unknowingly creating barriers to ministry?

_____

_____

_____

_____

_____

As the facilitator offers you some ways to evaluate your role as a leader, please write down your answers and thoughts in the workbook as we walk through this process together. Here are some ways to start your reflection:

- Ask yourself, "Am I ever a stumbling block to others or the ministry of Jesus Christ in the world?"

- When faced with a leadership decision are you conscious of the internal struggle the bishop illustrated in the book (quoted at the beginning of this session on page 11)?

- Reflect on the passage of scripture about Peter in Matthew 16:23. Could Jesus be saying the same things to us when we set our mind on human things like control and selfishness?

- When you are part of decision making at church, what guides you?

_____

_____

_____

_____

Unlocking the Power of Yes through the Forgiving Grace of Jesus Christ

The grace of God is going to help us overcome the obstacles preventing us from truly being a permission-giving leader and help us fully say *Yes* to following Jesus. In this next video, Rev. Jennifer Weekes-Klein will offer suggestions on spiritual practices that can move us from *No* to *Yes* through Jesus Christ.

Video: "Unlocking the Power of Yes: Becoming More Permission Giving"

Rev. Jennifer Weekes-Klein, senior pastor of Country Club United Methodist Church in Kansas City, shares the necessary personal, spiritual work that needs to be done in order to unlock the power of *Yes* in your life.

Openness Exercise

On the blank piece of paper in front of you, take a few moments to write down the *Nos* you want God to transform into *Yeses*. Take the time you need to really communicate with God. You can make it in the form of a prayer, a list of all the ways you want God to help you lead with trust and hope, a poem, or a drawing of *Nos*. The checklist of *Nos* from the session 1 worksheet and the following list are here to help you get started. These lists can help you recognize any negativity you might bring to ministry and want to give away to reach your full potential in God.

List of Negative Attitudes and Actions That Stifle Ministry
(Use this along with the session 1 checklist of *Nos* on page 6.)

- Fear—Fear of the unknown or change stops me from trying anything new.

- Passive aggressive behavior—I use disparaging or snide remarks, sabotage others, and so on.

- Negative attitude or thinking—Church is too old, too small, too poor, too _____.

- Unwillingness to help others—It will cost me too much; it's too hard; it's not my passion; or it's not for me.

- Harsh correction of others—That is not how I think it should be done; that is not how "we" do it.

- Body language—Disapproving glances, shaking of the head, crossing of the arms.

- Grudges—Holding on to past hurts, we sometimes let those color our decision and hurt others.

Prayer and Instructions

Once you have written down your confession or plea for God's help, crumple it up and hold it tightly in your fist. Please join together in this prayer of confession.

L: Lord, we confess our day-to-day failure to fully say *Yes* to you.

P: Lord, we confess to you.

L: Lord, we confess we often fail to love with all we have and are, often because we do not fully understand what loving means, often because we are afraid of risking ourselves.

P: Lord, we confess to you.

L: Lord, we confess we sometimes forget this church is yours.

P: We sometimes center our ministry on personal preferences and desires.

L: Lord, we confess that by silence and ill-considered words

P: we have built stumbling blocks to the creativity and passions of your people.

L: Lord, we confess that by selfishness and lack of sympathy

P: we have stifled generosity and missed opportunities to serve the least of these.

All: Holy Spirit, speak to us. Help us listen to your word of forgiveness so we might lessen our tight-fisted hold on leadership. Right now, help us open our hands to receive your grace. Allow us to become leaders of hope, innovation, and grace. Come, fill this moment and free us from sin. Amen.

(Adapted from #893 in *The United Methodist Hymnal*)

Holy Communion

You are invited now to unclench your fist and leave your confessions at the table of the Lord. Please come with open hands and hearts to receive this awe-inspiring gift of forgiveness and love. After you receive, please feel free to stay in prayer as long as you need. We will have a time of silence after receiving communion to allow us all to process the impact of God's freely given grace on our lives.

Time of Silent Reflection

During this time of silence, take a moment to fill in the answer to the following question. Have you begun letting go of the hurts or guilt about the *No* scenario you wrote down at the bottom of the session 1 worksheet? If not, keep the worksheet as a reminder to continue the process of letting go. The devotion guide we will introduce next will help you on your journey.

_____

_____

_____

_____

Permission-Giving Leader and Personal Devotion Introduction

In a culture of Yes, leaders are purveyors of hope. They believe in new life, new birth, and resurrection. They believe that God is at work in the minds and hearts of people, and that God is preparing people for ministries they never imagined. (95)

The book gives some example characteristics of permission-giving leaders. Here is a summary of those characteristics found on pages 95–99:

- They trust people and that God is at work in people and processes.
- They are responsible risk-takers.
- They grow their churches by multiplication and not just by addition.
- They know how to listen and get out of the way by opening options rather than closing them.

- They hold high expectations, are clear about the mission, and confident about the future.
- They seldom say *No* but ask encouraging questions to help discernment.
- They know exercising too much control limits creativity and capacity of staff and volunteers.
- They give space for people to answer their calling and value the initiatives of all people.
- They never go it alone.
- They have the ability to say *Yes* even to people who think differently from them.
- They develop habits that keep them freshly engaged with young people, new people, visitors, and those who do not yet belong to the church.

On this list, which characteristics are the most exciting and the most challenging to you?

Write down the ones you want to make a priority in your ministry. Keep these to help you develop your leadership in coming weeks.

_____

_____

_____

_____

_____

_____

_____

> Becoming a permission-giving leader is not an instantaneous transition. For this reason, you will find a seven-segment devotional at the back of this book. You are invited to invest more time after this study to keep your life centered on Christ and listen for God's continued call.

Guided Autonomy

Guided autonomy is the fine line between leaders who abandon their people and those who micromanage ministries. This balance happens when leaders guide and hold people accountable to the mission and vision of the church and support people to initiate and champion new ministries.

Video: "Hope in the Baking: Bridge Bread"

Lafayette Park United Methodist Church is an urban local church in one of the oldest parts of St. Louis. Through prayer and discernment, a small group of disciples began exploring the ministry and business of social enterprise and Bridge Bread was born.

Group Discussion and Accountability

When you think about the type of leader you are, do you tend toward the controlling, micro-managing, need-to-know-it-all side or are you closer to the leave-people-alone, abandon-and-never-follow-through side?

What is one thing you can do to find that balance point and lead with guided autonomy?

Name it, write it down, and then ask others here to gracefully hold you accountable to this goal. Keep these goals in mind along with the priorities for growing as a permission-giving leader, and work on them during your devotion time following this study.

_____

_____

_____

_____

_____

_____

_____

_____

_____

_____

_____

_____

_____

Brothers and sisters, I don't want you to be ignorant about spiritual gifts. You know that when you were Gentiles you were often misled by false gods that can't even speak. So I want to make it clear to you that no one says, "Jesus is cursed!" when speaking by God's Spirit, and no one can say, "Jesus is Lord," except by the Holy Spirit. There are different spiritual gifts but the same Spirit; and there are different ministries and the same Lord; and there are different activities but the same God who produces all of them in everyone. A demonstration of the Spirit is given to each person for the common good. A word of wisdom is given by the Spirit to one person, a word of knowledge to another according to the same Spirit, faith to still another by the same Spirit, gifts of healing to another in the one Spirit, performance of miracles to another, prophecy to another, the ability to tell spirits apart to another, different kinds of tongues to another, and the interpretation of the tongues to another. All these things are produced by the one and same Spirit who gives what he wants to each person.

Christ is just like the human body—a body is a unit and has many parts; and all the parts of the body are one body, even though there are many.

—1 Corinthians 12:1-12

Unleash a Culture of Yes

A culture of Yes *expects people to have ideas, gifts, and callings. It amplifies what works and encourages the passions and callings that already exist but which may remain unseen or hidden from view. (95)*

Core of the Book

According to Robert Schnase, the core of the *Just Say Yes!* book is "vibrant, fruitful, growing congregations have been willing to say *Yes* to things that declining congregations have said *No* to" (45).

Unleashing Systems: Creating a Culture Shift

This session, we will move from an emphasis on our personal leadership to the development of permission-giving systems in our church. This includes developing a framework to equip and encourage people to say *Yes* to God's call to serve using their gifts, talents, and passions. Let's start the work to unleash a culture of *Yes* here.

Video: "Unleashing Systems: Creating a Culture Shift"

Rev. Jim Downing, senior pastor of First United Methodist Church of Sedalia, shares how leaders can work to create a cultural shift from a *No* culture to a permission-giving culture.

Shifting from a *No* culture to an unleashed *Yes* culture is not easy. Over time, Rev. Jim Downing was able to lay a foundation changing the default from *No* to *Yes*. He now serves a culture-unleashing people for ministry. At its heart, this change is rooted in reminding people they are partnering with God for the work of offering hope.

Group Activity

Rev. Downing talks about three types of people: complainers, critics, and champions. Name some champions you have met.

_____

_____

_____

What about them unleashes others?

_____

_____

_____

What would shutting down the complaints department mean in our church and how could we make that happen?

_____

_____

_____

Permission-Giving Culture Development

In churches creatively saying *Yes*, like Rev. Downing's church, their systems encourage dreaming. How do we make this happen here? "Instead of the church council adopting a program and then convincing volunteers to implement it, a ministry begins with the sense of calling and enthusiasm among people at the margins, builds momentum, and then becomes recognized and adopted by the council" (9).

Role-Playing Exercise

Scenario 1

Narrator: A passionate young woman goes to the finance committee with an idea.

Young Woman: Recently, I saw a news report about Mexican people in poverty. No matter what I am doing, the faces of the people there just haunt me. It seems like God is calling me to lead a trip there to help, but since I have never done anything like this before I am coming to you for guidance.

Team Member (*putting on a sour face and abruptly shoving a piece of paper across to the young woman*): Well here is the church budget; if you can find money in there you can do it!

Narrator: This woman's spirit was crushed, and she stepped away from church for several years.

Scenario 2

Young Woman: Recently, I saw a news report about Mexican people in poverty. No matter what I am doing, the faces of the people there just haunt me. It seems like God is calling me to lead a trip there to help, but since I have never done anything like this before I am coming to you for guidance.

Team Member (*smiling*): Wow, thank you so much for sharing your passion! Can you tell me a little bit more about why you feel God is asking you to do this now?

Young Woman: Well, a while ago the pastor preached about how God gives us each gifts and talents to use to help others. Pastor also said sometimes we see a need in the world and then our gifts and talents will line up with that need. I am organized and have done international travel a lot with my job. My heart is breaking for these people, and I think we can offer hope.

Team Member: (*smiling*) I am sure Pastor will be thrilled you listened to the sermon. It also sounds like you are listening to God and willing to be the champion for this ministry.

Young Woman: Absolutely!

Team Member: Well, here are some things we can do to start. Why don't you line up some friends to pray about this mission. Also I believe the office of mission, service, and justice at our conference office has led some trips to Mexico. Let's find their number and get you in contact with them. After you get more information, how about we reserve a room after church and invite people to hear about your passion. The church budget is tight but with some creative fundraising nothing is impossible with God.

Young Woman: Oh thank you, I just needed a place to start and to hear from someone else that it is okay to think God really is talking to me.

Narrator: This time the young woman left excited. She was asked important questions to help her process. She was challenged to be the champion for this effort and to share it with others. She was encouraged to pray and to not expect all the money to come from the church budget. She was also affirmed in her call from God.

Sometimes *No* Is the Right Answer

Using all the insights we have gained so far we will create a structure to equip, strengthen, and unleash them to ministry. We must acknowledge that sometimes *No* is the right answer (87), but even better is having a framework to encourage people in their dreams.

Video: "Permission-Giving Leadership: When *No* Is the Right Answer"

Rev. Matt Miofsky, senior pastor of The Gathering in St. Louis, stresses that ideas that do not align with mission, priorities, and the spirit of the church are legitimate reasons to say *No*.

The key question to keep in mind as we move forward is "How can we say *Yes* to an element of people's ideas even when our initial, internal reaction is *No*?"

Team Missional Questions Development

To develop our framework for decision-making, Schnase gives some launching points (see table below). Please remember, this is not a time for brainstorming ministry ideas. This is the time to set a framework for encouraging the people in our midst to share their ideas and dreams for using the gifts and talents God has given them!

Missional Assumptions

1. Everyone has gifts for ministry.

2. God calls everyone to service and ministry.

3. The ministry of the Church should foster spiritual growth and discipleship.

4. The Church's mission is outward focused.

5. The work of the Church is to encourage people in their callings. (55-62)

Woods Chapel United Methodist Church's Three Questions

1. Does it align with the mission?

2. Who will do it?

3. How will it be funded?

Must be grounded in prayer, discernment, and calling. (75-76)

First United Methodist Church of Sedalia's Three Questions

1. Have you prayed about it?

2. Do you believe it is God's will for us at this time? (Timing is important: do we have the right resources for sustainability, the right alignment with priorities of the Church for this ministry at this time?)

3. Will it bring glory to Jesus Christ? (80)

Using the Questions

Now that we have our missional questions, turn back to the *No* example you wrote down at the end of session 1.

In groups of two to three revisit one or two of the *No* scenarios and replay it with our new mission questions.

How does the new framework change the conversation?

After a few minutes we will talk as a group about how these scenarios have changed with our increasingly permission-giving atmosphere.

Closing

At the beginning, we heard Jesus's promise that the Holy Spirit will always be with us as guide and teacher. We have started learning about and started becoming permission-giving leaders and church. As we close this study our work is not done, but we can be confident of the one we follow into the world. Remember Jesus said, "Peace I leave with you. My peace I give to you. I give to you not as the world gives. Don't be troubled or afraid" (John 14:27).

Leave in peace, and with the Spirit's power we will continue to say, *Yes*, Jesus, *Yes!* Let us say it together, *Yes*, Jesus, *Yes!*

You are invited to continue your growth as a permission-giving leader. Please dig into the devotion at the back of this guide. It holds tools for continuing this unleashing process. Work through the seven segments, and you will find yourself becoming a permission-giving leader in your congregation.

Notes

Use these pages to take notes, write out your thoughts, or sketch ideas.

Seven-Segment Devotional

Permission-Giving Leader Devotion Guide

An Introduction

During the uncover, unlock, unleash leader study, we scratched the surface of what it means to create a culture of **Yes**. This devotional guide is offered as a tool to deepen your relationship with the one who first gave you the ability to truly say *Yes*. Through the power of our creator God, our savior Jesus Christ, and our advocate the Holy Spirit, we can continue to grow into permission-giving leaders: leaders who are full of trust and hope; leaders who answer the call to love our neighbors and to go make disciples of Jesus Christ; leaders who encourage others to use their gifts and talents for the glory of God.

This devotion is designed to help unlock some of the obstacles holding you back from being an unleashed leader. Thankfully, God offers you multiple means of grace to unleash you for ministry in the world. Each session starts by naming a "lock" that may be holding you back from the fullness of leadership in Jesus Christ. Then we offer an "invitation to unlock" through the ultimate source in scripture and with insights found in Robert Schnase's book, *Just Say Yes! Unleashing People for Ministry*. Finally we offer "keys to unlock" including prayer, fasting, holy conferencing, and ideas for serving others. These keys are grace-filled opportunities to increasingly open up as a permission-giving leader. You can use this devotion for seven weeks, focusing on one session per week, or for an intense period of seven days. If you use this as a weekly devotion, here are some suggestions: reread the scripture daily and write about your insights in this book or a separate journal, spread the keys to unlock suggestions throughout the week, spend a day pondering and praying over the daily question, use the additional keys to unlock offered below, and make a plan to meet weekly with another team member to share your insights. By the end of this time of devotion, may you feel closer to God and understand more about yourself as a permission-giving leader.

Helpful Suggestions for Preparing for Your Time of Devotion
- Schedule time so you are not rushed.
- Find a quiet place without distractions.

- Have access to the Internet and/or CD player for some recommended activities.
- Have a Bible and a journal.
- Use the *Just Say Yes! Unleashing People for Ministry* book by Robert Schnase.
- Have cards to write personal notes.
- Have a white Christ candle.

Additional Keys to Unlock

If you have access to the Internet the Living Prayer Center (a ministry of The Upper Room) may be helpful (http://prayer-center.upperroom.org). This resource includes a variety of prayer methods and articles on prayer, along with help for discerning your spiritual type.

Then Jesus said to his disciples, "All who want to come after me must say no to themselves, take up their cross, and follow me. All who want to save their lives will lose them. But all who lose their lives because of me will find them."

—Matthew 16:24-25

Lock # 1

Distraction

Invitation to Unlock

God's Son, Jesus Christ, is the one who was preached among you by us—through me, Silvanus, and Timothy—he wasn't yes and no. In him it is always yes. All of God's promises have their yes in him. That is why we say Amen through him to the glory of God. God is the one who establishes us with you in Christ and who anointed us. God also sealed us and gave the Spirit as a down payment in our hearts. (2 Cor 1:19-22)

The Apostle Paul has a clarity of purpose and mission. He said *Yes* to Jesus and knows through Jesus all God's promises are *Yes*. This informs every decision he makes and gives him focus. His *Yes* gives him peace and grace to walk into the future. No matter what he faces—prison, illness, or persecution—the love of God keeps him clear about sharing this amazing gift with others.

A constant challenge for leaders is keeping everything in our lives focused on the mission and ministry of Jesus Christ. The world is moving so quickly and so many things compete for our attention. In this scripture, the Apostle Paul could easily be distracted from his purposes by the demands of life. He is forced to change his travel plans, and people begin to doubt him. They question if his words and actions line up with his ministry. He overcomes this questioning by reminding the people of Corinth that God's promises remain constant. The love and grace he continually offers the people comes from the one who is always faithful. As a leader, Paul faces everything with a clear knowledge of God's promises and focuses on his call to share the good news of Jesus Christ with others. His focus gives him clarity of purpose and helps him lead faithfully. No matter what the obstacle, he continually says *Yes* to Jesus!

Devotion Question

How are you keeping your focus on the purposes of Jesus Christ?

37

Keys to Unlock

These keys to unlock are to bless and enhance your devotion. They can be used immediately following the prayer or throughout daily life. They are offered as hopeful steps to help you become an increasingly permission-giving follower of Jesus Christ.

- Write down all the ways Jesus has said *Yes* in your life. What are God's promises to you? What are the "down payments" God has made on your heart (2 Cor 1:22)? Make this list a prayer of thanksgiving and end it with "through Jesus we give you all the glory God. Amen."

_____

_____

- At the end of the uncover, unlock, unleash leader study, you were anointed with oil. Reread the scripture above. Do you have the same sense Paul has of being anointed and commissioned for a special mission? What is your unique mission from God?

_____

_____

- When you start to pray, make note of all the distractions in your environment and in your mind. Make a plan to focus back on your time of prayer. Just as the Apostle Paul had plenty of distractions, our world continually tries to draw us away from the one who creates, saves, and sustains us. Here are some suggestions for focusing: Take time to write down all the things pulling your focus, and lift them specifically to God for guidance and blessing. Then take a moment to visualize the light of Christ settling on the place where you were sealed with oil during the study. Remember God has anointed you for leadership and lights your path.

_____

_____

_____

Prayer

Attentive God, thank you for participating in my life. Saying *Yes* to you each day, I will seek to avoid the distractions of this world and remain focused on bringing your love to people. Give me clarity in the midst of busyness and noise and the ability to lead faithfully. In the name of Jesus Christ. Amen.

By faith Abraham obeyed when he was called to go out to a place that he was going to receive as an inheritance. He went out without knowing where he was going.

By faith he lived in the land he had been promised as a stranger. He lived in tents along with Isaac and Jacob, who were coheirs of the same promise. He was looking forward to a city that has foundations, whose architect and builder is God.

By faith even Sarah received the ability to have a child, though she herself was barren and past the age for having children, because she believed that the one who promised was faithful. So descendants were born from one man (and he was as good as dead). They were as many as the number of the stars in the sky and as countless as the grains of sand on the seashore. All of these people died in faith without receiving the promises, but they saw the promises from a distance and welcomed them. They confessed that they were strangers and immigrants on earth. People who say this kind of thing make it clear that they are looking for a homeland. If they had been thinking about the country that they had left, they would have had the opportunity to return to it. But at this point in time, they are longing for a better country, that is, a heavenly one. Therefore, God isn't ashamed to be called their God—he has prepared a city for them.

—Hebrews 11:8-16

Lock #2

Apathy

Invitation to Unlock

You know I held back nothing that would be helpful so that I could proclaim to you and teach you both publicly and privately in your homes. You know I have testified to both Jews and Greeks that they must change their hearts and lives as they turn to God and have faith in our Lord Jesus. Now, compelled by the Spirit, I'm going to Jerusalem. I don't know what will happen to me there. What I do know is that the Holy Spirit testifies to me from city to city that prisons and troubles await me. But nothing, not even my life, is more important than my completing my mission. This is nothing other than the ministry I received from the Lord Jesus: to testify about the good news of God's grace. (Acts 20:20-24)

Everything about the Apostle Paul's life changed once he meets and commits to following Jesus Christ. His language exudes a passion and devotion to God. He even considers his life nothing but a tool for offering the grace of God for others. Paul says no matter what obstacles he faces, he is willing to do it for the cause of Jesus Christ. The message is worthy of any sacrifice. This is what Schnase refers to as imperative. "*Imperative* refers to drive, passion, momentum, excitement, and desire that motivates ministry" (46). He goes on to share how

[leaders and] congregations with a sense of imperative believe that the work of Christ is absolutely necessary, vital to life and rebirth, and that inviting people into the spiritual life is something that must be done. They operate under the mandates of Christ, the imperatives that lace the teachings of Jesus: "Go.... Teach.... Heal.... Welcome.... Give.... Serve.... Pray.... Do.... Love.... Follow." (47)

Devotion Question

Do you have imperative drive for the mission and purposes of Christ?

41

Keys to Unlock

These keys to unlock are to bless and enhance your devotion. They can be used immediately following the prayer or throughout daily life. They are offered as hopeful steps to help you become an increasingly permission-giving follower of Jesus Christ.

- Take a few minutes to reread pages 45–49 in *Just Say Yes!* under the heading, "A Sense of Imperative." Thinking about the asthma example in this section, imagine the feeling: "You can breathe again, all fear is gone, and there's new energy and vitality" (47). With this sense, practice the following breath prayer in a place of quiet and comfort. First, take a deep breath in and then hold it. Pay attention to your body and hold it until you are desperate for breath. Then repeatedly, passionately breathe in the name of God, and then breathe out your plea for help. For example, breathe in saying, "creator God" and breathe out saying, "breathe life in me." Here are phrases to help you begin: "Creator God, breathe life in me." "Lord Jesus, save me." "Holy Spirit, make me yours."

- Write down your passions. How are you using them for the mission and purposes of Jesus Christ?

_____

_____

_____

- Remember a story of how Jesus grabbed hold of your life and find a way to share it with someone this week. It can be a note of encouragement, a call, or a coffee time to share.

Prayer

Active God, help me create imperative in my life and ministry. Remind me what it means to passionately follow you and long to share your good news with others. Instill in me overflowing love and hope that will positively impact your people. In the name of Jesus Christ. Amen.

"I have spoken these things to you while I am with you. The Companion, the Holy Spirit, whom the Father will send in my name, will teach you everything and will remind you of everything I told you.

"Peace I leave with you. My peace I give you. I give to you not as the world gives. Don't be troubled or afraid."

—John 14:25-27

Lock #3

Fear

Invitation to Unlock

I am the LORD your God, / who grasps your strong hand, / who says to you, / Don't fear; I will help you. (Isa 41:13)

You didn't receive a spirit of slavery to lead you back again into fear, but you received a Spirit that shows you are adopted as his children. With this Spirit, we cry, "Abba, Father." (Rom 8:15)

God didn't give us a spirit that is timid but one that is powerful, loving, and self-controlled. (2 Tim 1:7)

Throughout scripture, in both Old and New Testaments, God calls us from fear toward trust. Permission-giving leaders are grounded in trust and hope. This allows them to be creative and encouraging to others. Out of this encouragement, innovation and dreaming happens and things change. Change can bring us back to fear if we are not careful and intentional to grow in faith. Schnase's book asks an important question about why we struggle with change.

> Why do people resist change and reject new ideas even when they know that the old habits, attitudes, and systems are holding them back from doing greater good? [Leadership author] Ronald Heifetz says that people do not fear change; they fear loss. People fear the grief that comes with losing what has been familiar, reliable, and known; habits, values, and attitudes—even those that have been barriers to progress and unhelpful for the mission—are part of one's identity, and changing them challenges how we define ourselves." (7–8)

Fear is powerful, but the love and grace of Jesus Christ can overcome the greatest of fear. Putting our trust in Jesus Christ is the key to being leaders who continually are willing to risk for the glory of God's kingdom.

Devotion Question

How do you overcome fear of change and loss?

Keys to Unlock

These keys to unlock are to bless and enhance your devotion. They can be used immediately following the prayer or throughout daily life. They are offered as hopeful steps to help you become an increasingly permission-giving follower of Jesus Christ.

- Pick one of the scripture passages from above to use in a *lectio divina* prayer exercise. You will read the text three times. During the first reading, pay attention to what word or phrase takes your focus. Write down this word or phrase. During the second reading, focus on what images and thoughts this word or phrase brings to mind. Take some time to draw an image from your thoughts, journal, or go for a walk praying for God to speak to you. During the third reading, read it out loud and hear any challenge God may be giving you through the text. What do you need to do or say to faithfully live into this message from God's word? Leave this time of prayer with comfort and confidence in your connection with the living God.

_____

_____

_____

- Think of a time when you were afraid. How did God help you overcome the fear? When change has happened in church, what losses were the hardest for you to accept? Why?

_____

_____

_____

- Take a few moments to rest in the constancy of God's love and grace for you. Fear can be overcome with the assurance of God's forever faithfulness. Listen to or play a song that helps you feel the faithfulness of God. If you have access to the Internet, a possible song is "One Thing Remains" by Bethel Music, performed by Jesus Culture.

Prayer

Steadfast God, bring me into your presence in moments of fear. May I trust you more faithfully in moments of change and loss. Help me to see your creative work in this world and be excited about the possibilities you place in my path. With certainty in you, allow me to lead others well in moments of change. In the name of Jesus Christ. Amen.

Therefore, as a prisoner for the Lord, I encourage you to live as people worthy of the call you received from God. Conduct yourselves with all humility, gentleness, and patience. Accept each other with love, and make an effort to preserve the unity of the Spirit with the peace that ties you together. You are one body and one spirit, just as God also called you in one hope. There is one Lord, one faith, one baptism, and one God and Father of all, who is over all, through all, and in all.

—Ephesians 4:1-6

Negativity

Invitation to Unlock

Don't let any foul words come out of your mouth. Only say what is helpful when it is needed for building up the community so that it benefits those who hear what you say. (Eph 4:29)

These words are crucial to hear and repeat today. Words hold great power to tear down or to inspire. Think of the dramatic difference between a time when someone hurt you with words and a time when someone used words to lift you up. When we speak negative words, we may be discouraging or stopping the passions and gifts of others in our midst.

The *No* person looks for problems, and then focuses exclusively on how to fix them.... "I serve a dysfunctional church," a pastor says. "I could never get my people to do that." [Or] "That would never work here," a layperson laments. "Our church doesn't have enough people or money." The repetition and reinforcement of these negative perceptions create a self-fulfilling prophecy. Leaders who focus exclusively on what's broken ... and what can't happen foster an environment that makes change impossible. (95)

Devotion Question

Author Robert Schnase challenges us to ask, "What if we believed that we have exactly enough people and resources to fulfill the ministry God is calling us to today?" (95).

Keys to Unlock

These keys to unlock are to bless and enhance your devotion. They can be used immediately following the prayer or throughout daily life. They are offered as hopeful steps to help you become an increasingly permission-giving follower of Jesus Christ.

- Recall from the *Just Say Yes!* study the video, "Unleashing Systems: Creating a Cultural Shift." (If you have access to the DVD or streamed video clip, you might take a look at it again.) In this video, Rev. Jim Downing says there are two common "rails" churches operate on: "we've always done it this way" (stuck in the past) and "we've never done it that way before" (fear of failure). In his ministry context, they created a mission jar and anytime anyone started to say anything negative like these two phrases they paid one dollar for missions. Create a jar for yourself and place one dollar in for missions any time negative words come from your mouth. Positivity and hope will become a habit.

- What negativity do you carry in your heart about the ministries or people in your congregation? It is nearly impossible to stay negative when you come face to face with the light of Christ. Get a white candle and find a quiet and preferably dark space to light the candle. Before you turn out the room light, light the candle and read Matthew 5:14-16: "You are the light of the world. A city on top of a hill can't be hidden. Neither do people light a lamp and put it under a basket. Instead, they put it on top of a lampstand, and it shines on all who are in the house. In the same way, let your light shine before people, so they can see the good things you do and praise your Father who is in heaven." Believe deep in your heart this is the light of Christ burning away any negativity you carry. Christ's light is the hope, joy, and love you will carry into the world with you. Stay in an attitude of meditation as long as you feel connected to the light of Christ.

_____

_____

_____

- Take a few moments to read the "instead of" questions on pages 65–66 of *Just Say Yes!* Which strike you as the most challenging and the most empowering?

_____

_____

_____

Prayer

Inspiring God, may I rely on your hope in moments of difficulty and negativity. Help me to speak words that build up rather than tear down people. Give me your joy each day so I can offer hope to people who are worried or afraid in this world. In the name of Jesus Christ. Amen.

But the fruit of the Spirit is love, joy, peace, patience, kindness, goodness, faithfulness, gentleness, and self-control. There is no law against things like this. Those who belong to Christ Jesus have crucified the self with its passions and its desires.

If we live by the Spirit, let's follow the Spirit. Let's not become arrogant, make each other angry, or be jealous of each other.

—Galatians 5:22-26

Lock #5

Selfishness

Invitation to Unlock

Therefore, if there is any encouragement in Christ, any comfort in love, any sharing in the Spirit, any sympathy, complete my joy by thinking the same way, having the same love, being united, and agreeing with each other. Don't do anything for selfish purposes, but with humility think of others as better than yourselves. Instead of each person watching out for their own good, watch out for what is better for others. (Phil 2:1-4)

When we make ourselves the focus of our decision making, we push Christ from the center of our lives. The scripture talks of the difference between selfish purposes and the encouraging, loving, joyful purposes of Christ. Schnase says this about our struggles with selfishness, "We align the ministries with our preferences rather than discerning what aligns with Christ's work. We become protective, defensive, controlling, and territorial. We say *No*" (9). When we make it all about us, we ask "'What's in it for me?'... 'How does this affect me? Will I benefit from it?' And most importantly, 'What will I have to do? What will it cost me?'"(10).

When we ask questions like these, how is the love of God evident in our lives and leadership? Do our actions show we are "watch[ing] out for what is better for others"?

Devotion Question

How are you sharing your time, resources, gifts, and passions to show your love of God and neighbor?

Keys to Unlock

These keys to unlock are to bless and enhance your devotion. They can be used immediately following the prayer or throughout daily life. They are offered as hopeful steps to help you become an increasingly permission-giving follower of Jesus Christ.

- Serving others is the best way to counter selfishness. Create a graph matrix like the one described in *Just Say Yes!* (see 57–59 and the example below). On the left side of the graph list needs you see in the world. Along the bottom write your personal interests, gifts, passions, and talents. Find the intersection. Are there others doing this type of ministry you can join or should you start a prayer of discernment around using your gifts? If you are uncertain about the gifts God has given you, please take some time to do a spiritual gifts inventory. Try this one from the United Methodist tradition or use one from your tradition: http://www.umc.org/what-we-believe/spiritual-gifts-online-assessment.

		Writing	Generosity	Good with Children
Needs I See in the World That Break My Heart	**Illiteracy in Children**	I could offer my skills to write about the needs. Possibly educate people at church and beyond.	I could donate books to after school Christian reading/tutoring ministries.	I could volunteer to read with kids at an after school reading ministry.
	Kids in Foster Care	I could offer my skills to write about the needs. Possibly educate people at church and beyond.	I could donate items to ministries that help kids in transition.	I could train to do respite care for foster care families.
		Writing	Generosity	Good with Children
		My Passion, Gifts, and Talents		

- This week, find a way to intentionally show the love of Jesus Christ to others through service. This is not about us—this is about giving thanks for what God has done for us. By serving others, we will be living "the pattern of gracious love" we read above.

- Humility Prayer—If you typically pray sitting up, consider praying on your knees. If you normally pray on your knees, consider praying prostrate (lay with your face down). Increase your physical expression of humility and offer a prayer such as the Wesley Covenant prayer (contemporary version) from the Methodist tradition or one of your own.

Prayer

Generous God, thank you for all you give to me daily. All that I am and all that I have are gifts from you. I long to model my life after your example of humility through Jesus Christ. The life, death and resurrection of Jesus are testaments to how willing you are to give extravagantly to your people. Help me focus on loving and serving others in my decision making and in our church ministries. In the name of Jesus Christ. Amen.

"I am the true vine, and my Father is the vineyard keeper. He removes any of my branches that don't produce fruit, and he trims any branch that produces fruit so that it will produce even more fruit. You are already trimmed because of the word I have spoken to you. Remain in me, and I will remain in you. A branch can't produce fruit by itself, but must remain in the vine. Likewise, you can't produce fruit unless you remain in me."

—John 15:1-4

Lock #6

Control

Invitation to Unlock

As Jesus walked alongside the Galilee Sea, he saw two brothers, Simon, who is called Peter, and Andrew, throwing fishing nets into the sea, because they were fishermen. "Come, follow me," he said, "and I'll show you how to fish for people." Right away, they left their nets and followed him. (Matt 4:18-20)

When we are called to follow Jesus, we do not know where this may lead us. This takes control out of our hands. Following Jesus means first remembering you are a follower and then a leader. This takes faith in the one you follow. "The essence of faith is captured in the words that describe Abraham's obedience to God's call, 'He went out without knowing where he was going' (Heb 11:8)" (5).

It is easy to feel a need to hold the reigns tight when you are a leader. Yet a need for control makes it nearly impossible to truly *follow Jesus*. When we want to constantly have the final say in decision-making, believe it has to be done by us, and have to know everything, we often say *No*. Recognizing God's call and gifting of other people means there will be ministries happening beyond one person's control. Permission-giving leaders know relinquishing control can be messy but also realize saying *Yes* to Jesus is worth it.

"Unleashing people for ministry sets a church on an unpredictable path. It multiplies ministry. It interrupts the business as usual. *Yes* unleashes the wild, raw nature of God" (90).

The disciples threw down their nets, their way of life, to follow Jesus into an uncertain future. That act of faith allowed them to witness the extraordinary good news of the life, death, and resurrection of Jesus Christ. Their willingness to follow helped the good news reach us today.

Devotion Question

What will your leadership legacy be? Will you be the one who "killed ideas, closed down initiatives, curtailed the ministries of energetic and passionate people"? Or, will you "be the person God works through rather than the person God has to work around"? (13).

Keys to Unlock

These keys to unlock are to bless and enhance your devotion. They can be used immediately following the prayer or throughout daily life. They are offered as hopeful steps to help you become an increasingly permission-giving follower of Jesus Christ.

- Consider trying a Wesley fast, which comes from the Methodist tradition. Feel free to use another form of fasting if Methodism is not your tradition. "The Wesley Fast, traditionally observed, begins with dinner on Thursday evening and continues until tea time on Friday. Time and energy that would have been consumed in eating is offered for deeper prayer, meditation, and works of charity and compassion. When for health reasons such a fast is not advisable, persons are encouraged to adjust the fast to their personal needs. Please remember to drink plenty of juice and water" (http://www.umc.org/who-we-are/call-to-prayer-and-fasting). The time you spend fasting can be used to focus on faith and your dependence on God. It can help reorient your leadership from control to following and believing God is gifting others with ideas for ministries. If a medical reason makes a food fast unsafe, please consider refraining from other activities such as social media, talking, and so on.

- Find a person in the congregation you trust to talk with about your leadership style. Have them help you discern times when they have witnessed you try to hold onto control. Pray with them and ask them to hold you accountable for leading with obedience to Christ's mandates and not your own.

- In addition to meeting with others to talk about leadership, you can form a covenant or accountability group. Each meeting you could share joys and concerns, where you have seen God moving in your life, and your current struggles related to faithfulness.

Prayer

Empowering God, you have given me amazing opportunities to lead in your name. Remind me not to seek to control or micromanage ministry. I never want to be in the way of your work in the world. Remind me daily that I follow you and you are worthy of all my faith. Out of this faith, help me partner with you to unleash people for ministry. In the name of Jesus Christ. Amen.

Now the eleven disciples went to Galilee, to the mountain where Jesus told them to go. When they saw him, they worshipped him, but some doubted. Jesus came near and spoke to them, "I've received all authority in heaven and on earth. Therefore, go and make disciples of all nations, baptizing them in the name of the Father and of the Son and of the Holy Spirit, teaching them to obey everything that I've commanded you. Look, I myself will be with you every day until the end of this present age."

—Matthew 28:16-20

Lock #7

Discouragement

Let's hold on to the confession of our hope without wavering, because the one who made the promises is reliable. And let us consider each other carefully for the purpose of sparking love and good deeds. Don't stop meeting together with other believers, which some people have gotten into the habit of doing. Instead, encourage each other, especially as you see the day drawing near. (Heb 10:23-25)

A discouraged congregation will hear more *Nos* than *Yeses*. The people will be less likely to dream and more likely to focus on themselves. They will show less love, do less service, and be more afraid of change. Yet this kind of culture can change with hope. Hebrews tells us we can have hope because God's promises are reliable. We are called to "spark love and good deeds" in each other as followers of Jesus Christ. Permission-giving leaders have hope and they encourage others!

Encouragement literally means "to fill with courage and strength of purpose, to hearten, to give heart." Encouragement refers to the action of giving someone support, confidence, and hope.... to inspire and motivate.... temboldens rather than restrains, empowers rather than limits, stimulates people to move forward rather than to retreat.... Real encouragement means helping people say *Yes* to God." (112–13)

Encouragement not only lifts up the individual but it builds up the entire community of faith.

Devotion Question

How do we stop discouraging and become encouragers?

Keys to Unlock

These keys to unlock are to bless and enhance your devotion. They can be used immediately following the prayer or throughout daily life. They are offered as hopeful steps to help you become an increasingly permission-giving follower of Jesus Christ.

- Spend some focused time in prayer for others in your congregation. Before you pray the following prayer, think of specific people in the congregation you want to lift to God. Who needs encouragement for tough life situations or encouragement to answer a call to ministry, and who longs for connection and purpose? *Encouraging and empowering God, your word tells us we are part of your son's body. Help us remember, "The whole body grows from him, as it is joined and held together by all the supporting ligaments. The body makes itself grow in that it builds itself up with love as each one does its part" (Eph 4:16). We need your help to grow. We need your help to properly use the gifts you have given each of us. We need your help to encourage each other in love. Please hear this urgent plea to encourage _____, who is in desperate need of hope. Please hear my hopeful plea for you to help _____, to answer their call to ministry. Please hear my grateful plea to empower _____, who needs a place to connect, a purpose, and longs to serve. I praise you God for this opportunity to lift my fellow brothers and sisters to you with confidence my prayers will be heard. May your will be done in this place. Amen.*

- Permission-giving leaders spend time with others. They help people at all stages of faith to listen to God, "to follow their callings, explore ideas they are curious about, and experiment with new approaches" (99). Who is the first person that comes to mind when you think of someone at church who needs encouragement to follow his or her God-given dreams? Consider inviting him or her to coffee or writing him or her a note of encouragement. Here are some thoughts on encouraging others:
    - Pray with them and for them.
    - Help them connect with others who might have similar passions, invite them to do a spiritual gifts inventory, and ask questions to help them dream.
    - Encourage them to do a graph like the one mentioned in lock #5 of this devotional guide if they want help finding their purpose.

_____

_____

_____

Prayer

Encouraging God, lift me up in moments I become discouraged in ministry. Allow my leadership to be centered on loving you and my neighbors. Give me courage, strength of purpose, and heart so I can share this with others. Inspire and motivate me to remain a person of *Yes*, one who helps others say *Yes* to you. In the name of Jesus Christ. Amen.